ttle Book of Answers

# Why Do We Celebrate?

Written by Ben Smith

History

# Vital Vocabulary

famous scientist

12

first man in space

8

RST MAN ON THE MOON
UNITED STATES

Wilbur et Orville WRIGHT
50F
POSTE AERIENNE
EMPIRE CENTRAFRICAIN



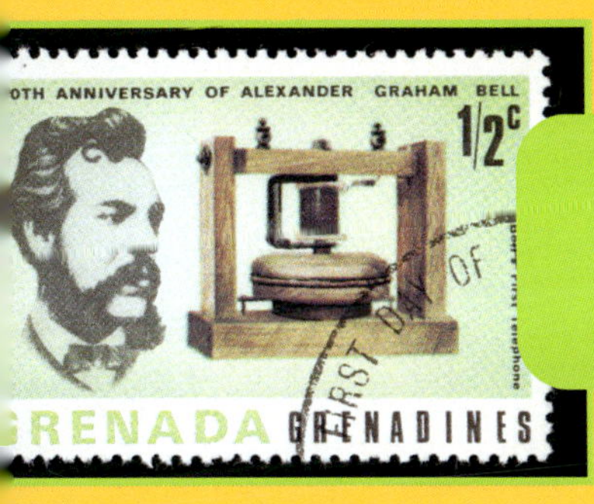
0TH ANNIVERSARY OF ALEXANDER GRAHAM BELL
1/2c
RENADA GRENADINES



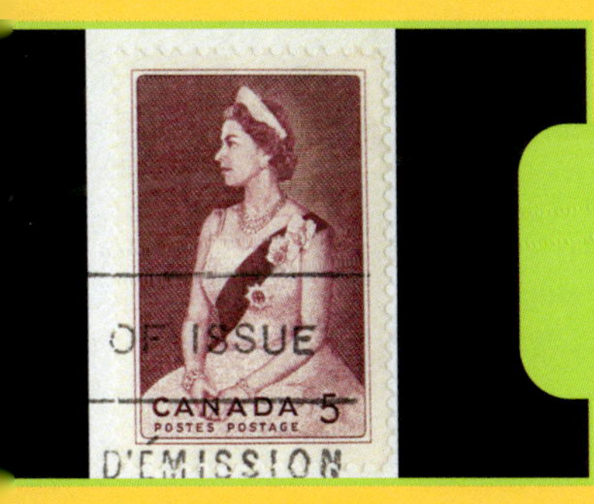
OF ISSUE
CANADA 5
POSTES POSTAGE
D'EMISSION

We celebrate because
he invented the telephone.
He is on a stamp.

Alexander Graham Bell invented the telephone.

We celebrate because they flew the first plane. They are on a stamp.

The Wright brothers flew the first plane.

We celebrate because
he was the first person
to go into space.
He is on a stamp.

Yuri Gagarin was the first man in space.

We celebrate because he was the first person to walk on the moon. He is on a stamp.

Neil Armstrong was the first man on the moon.

We celebrate because
he was a famous scientist.
He is on a stamp.

Albert Einstein was a famous scientist.

We celebrate because
she was the Queen of England
for more than 50 years.

| Stamp | Person |
|---|---|
|  | Alexander Graham Bell |
|  | Wright Brothers |
|  | Yuri Gagarin |
|  | Neil Armstrong |
| 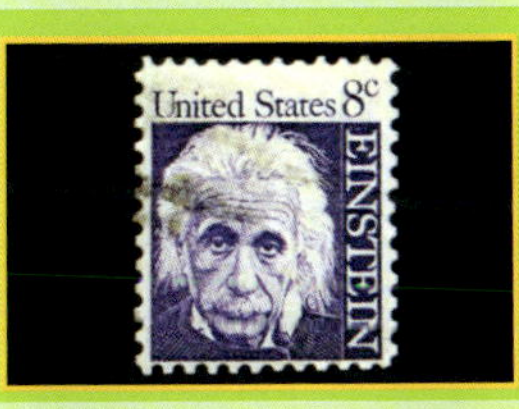 | Albert Einstein |
|  | Queen of England |

# Critical Thinking

Who are these people?
Why do you think we should celebrate them?